Doorways to the Light

Published by Caro Publishing

Doorways to the Light
© 2004 Caroline Hope
All rights reserved

ISBN **0-9544918-1-5**

Published by
Caro Publishing
Court Farm House,
Little Witcombe,
Gloucester
GL3 4TU

caro9009@aol.com

Printed by
Windmill Graphics
PO Box 11,
Stroud,
Glos.
GL5 5BH
www.windmillgraphics.co.uk

All the proceeds of the sale of this book will be donated to

For grieving children and their families

Bayshill Road, Cheltenham
dedicated
to all families on a journey
living with loss

Acknowledgements.
Some of these poems have appeared in the following publications:
Harlequin; Quantum Leap; Poetry Church; Peace & Freedom
Cover Paintings by Caroline Hope

Here I am!
I stand at the door and knock.
If anyone hears my voice and opens the door,
I will come in and eat with him, and he with me.

Revelation 3 v20

CONTENTS

9	**body**		36	The one
	Breath		37	Haiku
10	Walking meditation		38	Education
	Haiku		39	Where I come from
11	Standing meditation		40	The Service
12	Yoga		41	Meeting
13	Chakra			
14	Fore given moments		**42**	**soul**
	Haiku			The bench V
15	Step		43	The walk
	GAP II		44	Marks
16	Grave amuse		45	Sea
			46	Door II
18	**mind**		47	Under cover of darkness
	The attempt		48	Summer comes
19	Waters		49	Test
	Two haiku		50	The portal
21	The collection		51	Silence
22	Blasphemy and Remembrance			String theory
24	Roll the stone		52	Stone
25	Switch		53	The cloud of unknowing
26	Judgement Day		54	Route Finder
27	Haiku		55	Sea storm
28	Snake		56	The past
29	Airbrushing the Sun Installation		57	Wind
30	Butterfly Wing		58	Cry
31	Haiku		59	Abraham and Isaac
32	The sacrifice		60	Leaving Home
33	A Brief History of Time and the Secret of the Universe Explained		62	Surrender
			63	Soul light
	Haiku		64	Go flow
34	Sunday Morning in Bishop's Cleeve			

65 dreams & visions
    Door
66   Tent
67   Empty Rooms
68   Travellers
69   Door III
70   Graduation
72   Attack
73   Mantle
74   Dreams
76   The valley Path
77   Held in God's gaze: The chase

78 angels
    Stone Butterfly
79   Awake
80   Loneliness
81   Companion
82   Net
83   Ghost
    Haiku
84   Beach Life
85   November 11ᵗʰ
86   The golden marigold
87   Cufflinks
88   You are there
89   Haiku
90   Who blesses the vicar?

91 love and fear
    This word
92   Tree worship
93   Sheep
94   Ode to a Deer

95   Duck
96   Home Flight
97   Summer afternoon
98   Roe Deer
    Haiku
99   Tenderness
100 Love lost
101 Memories
102 Christmas Story
104 I am in peace
    Haiku

105 still moments
    Three Haiku
106 Evening
107 Stillness
108 Cat
    Horse
109 Sunday moment
110 Lunchtime at Stanton
111 Two Haiku
112 The host
    Haiku
113 Sunday Morning
    Haiku
114 Spring
115 Starry night
    Haiku

116 revelations
Come alive
Door IV
117 Snowdrops
118 Tiercel
119 Dear David
120 Blackbird
121 Air freshener
122 God loves me?
123 Forgiveness
124 All That Is
126 Stairs
127 Cancer cure
128 A transfiguration
129 I will follow
130 Mike's Trinity
131 Tread lightly
132 A poem for all people
133 Held in God's Gaze: Reprise
134 Tiercel II

body

Breath

I am
a breath away.

I am
here, in your breath.

Walking meditation

Rhythmical step
one before
one after
one taken
one replaced.
Rhythmic reflections
come up
to meet
the foot
intangible
moments
of transference.
Earth crumbling
air
breathless lung
gasp
heart steadfast
energy exchange
heat
vaporize
molecule shifting
transference,
out of time,
into eternity.

Haiku

when we walk in the
fullness of time there is
sufficiency

Standing meditation

Two feet
equally placed
heels below
hips
parallel
toes
wide spaced
pelvic
alignment
abdomen
supporting spinal arrangement
stacked vertebrae
the breath
lifting ribs
expansion
contraction
rising
falling
head balance
eyes lowered
unfocussed
arms at rest
fingers unclenched
rising
falling
inspire
expire
breath
in stillness
forever
here

Yoga

Come back to breath
in stillness
standing in patient fortitude
like the holiness of a tree,
unfurling, by degree,
in silent stretch from
budding tip
the fullness of bodily sense
empty of thought;
curling from anchoring roots
correctly aligned
into inner perfection.
Letting go, mindfully,
the resistance,
leaf spirits move in the wind
and translate muscle tension,
giving up in the breath;
standing empty
between heaven and earth
here now
in the sound,
is God.
And then stepping out
into living air,
heavy with scent
and warm expectation, is
breath turned into love.

Chakra

Breath insinuates earth,
rooting basal shoots feel for living waters
and energy divining an upward growth
onto sacral plane.
Desirous temptations as sap rises
and fear finds no purchase
in the power of love,
and then no turning back
to express God's glory,
guided by visioning wisdom.

Heaven's blessings pour down
on the lotus,
incarnating fulfilment
in mind, body and soul.
This light of consciousness
floods through a joining of heaven and earth.
Awake sleeping serpent.

Fore Given Moments

How dull-witted I appear to be!
How slow, how wrapped in vanity!
What goes before consciousness, I'll never know;
I always miss the magic moment, the incorrupt show.
If only my senses were quick to savour
I could always taste the present time, and know it's flavour.
My ears would disentangle primaeval noises
and turn them into celestial voices.
Eden's garden would flood the air with heavenly scents
and I could bathe in the purity of ecstatic moments.
If only my vision could reach infinity, then, eye bright,
I would see the beginning and end of all in cosmic light.
And if my senses were not so dull and slow,
my fingers could touch your uncreated soul.
And yet how joyous to be able to linger and capture
these forgiven moments, and experience rapture.

Haiku

iced east wind
slices flesh from cheek bone
knife tempered by sun

Step

He is
a step away.

He is
here, in your step

GAP II

Awake!

Nothing happens
in the gap.

The pre-sent impulse
vibrantly alive
with pious possibilities
before consciousness
takes it from the
sacred space
and it is clarified
deep within.

Grave amuse

Grave rows of churchyard stones,
trimmed with flouncing posies
as a florist's window out of tune
with the soft misted wintry moon.

Is there resurrection
in this lurid perfection?

Let me be buried
where the hungry earth alone
will share fruit of my bones.

Let my flesh rot
where the worm can take meat
and writhing maggot silently feast.

Let me lie
where springing deer may feed
on verdant pastures gone to seed.

Let me be interred
in a woodland glade
where my corpse will be
of some use to a tree.

Let my body lie
between earth and sky,
an alchemy released
and life increased.

Scatter my ashes, burn my flesh

but let me not die a florist's death,
a hardcased, regimented, gaudy death,
a wrapped in cellophane, unrotting death,
an out of order,
unresurrected,
disconnected death.

mind

The attempt

Attempt with intent
everyday intend your attempt
and believe
one day
you will achieve

Waters

Holy messages contained
as sacred waters separated.
Walled enclosures with doorways to heaven;
Healing powers thus removed from earth.
Reach out to pull some in -
this is the way.
Scatter a little holy water,
hope to touch;
swim as one or drown in the flood.
This is the way.

He did not come to preach separation.
He did not come to teach
dry stone walling in your mind.
He came to destroy barriers.

When these walls crumble
waters will flow
waters will flow
waters will flow.

Messages met and mingled
here on earth
becoming from many fountains
one all consuming end
to flow out
earth nourishing waters
not contained and not lost
but one living return
to the cycle of life.

Let all waters be met

in birthing heaven
on living earth
and in the all consuming deathly deep.

The eternal circle;
living waters.

Two Haiku

overflowing waters
race in spate to meet their maker;
ocean depth

hungry stream replenished;
many diverse beginnings
one all consuming end

The collection

Ridged and furrowed prayers
uttered behind averted expressions locked
inside small doorways to heaven.

Today we could collect some smiles!
Scrape them off our lips,
release them into the aisles,
Sweep them out of the world church door
let them fly to the Middle East,
and wing beat earth with their peace.

Blasphemy and Remembrance

Not in disregard for the church iconic splendour.
Not in the repetitive horror of the miserable Christ bearing the cross;
the marble knee polished smooth by continual touch and tear.
Not in the failure to feel holy before Mary's seven daggered
pierced and statuesque heart;
but in ourselves the blasphemy comes.
The drawing away, the glossing over,
the hurrying on to place and time,
the distracted irritation, the forgetful consumption,
the gluttony without the remembrance:

"Take this bread and eat.
This is my body in yours…"
And as you do so remember
for as this bread nourishes your body,
so the remembrance nourishes your soul.

"Take this wine and drink.
This is my blood flowing in your veins…"
And as you do so remember
for as the wine refreshes your body
so your remembrance refreshes your soul.

In the forgetfulness of gluttony
only remember the crowd's clamour
and hunger for the spirit.

Will the preacher's voice reach
across the empty marches?
His words are taken and passed back.
So few words shared, made much.
Bread for the soul. Fish for the mind.
Pass it amongst you; share it out.
No fragment is wasted.

Hungering before the preacher
the starving spirit cries out.

Did you hear his words?

"We heard. We collected a fragment
that was passed amongst us
it fed our body it nourished our soul
and in the stillness of remembrance
we felt God's love in God's presence.
We ate from the increase."

Roll the stone

Roll the stone away
from the cave of your mind
await there the dark guilty tunnels
empty as night
disappearing into unfathomable depths,
a fearsome flight.

Ghostly dawn light falteringly curls
insinuating, misting, clouding through.
The sweet notes of the lark,
heralding the morn,
are caught, softly insistent,
outside the dark deafening silence within.

Attend, because in that moment of wonder
you may turn to see the sunrise
catching the stone,
sparking the glittering quartz,
flooding through the cave
into the heart of it.

The spark ignites and purifies.
Created space manifests
inside and around all living cells
allowing vibration.

You stand all powerful
greeting the light
secure in the centre
of the open cave.

Switch

Unconnected jet lagged consciousness,
behind the screen the desire screams for vision.
In the silence, the utter black, a recollection stirs
a lost memory.
Then watch the thought, the desire, the emotion
and however false the ego makes the intent,
however much the mind tugs
incessantly for the next event,
in that anxious gap
resolve not to respond,
resolve, however faint,
To be there, be present, be a saint.

Judgement Day

When the day comes
that you are asked
how you spent your time,
will your answer be
that your life was a day dream,
your reality uncertain,
your comfort make believe,
your thoughts a distraction?
Or will your answer be
that you spent your life
in loving remembrance,
attending every impulse,
every sacred second;
that all the world was a reminder
to stay in this place, in reverence;
not one second was lost,
not one second wasted?

Will you also wonder
does madness come?
The mind reeling in blank unknowing,
the only thought being
I don't know who I am any more.
There is only desperation for memory - any memory,
for it was easier to live in daydreams, than this liberty.

Walking in stillness,
the trees' omnipresence in silent
command of respect,
namaste they whisper,
as the breeze
takes their leaves
to remind, to remind me.

When I don't know who I am anymore,
when I feel the worldly flood of rage,
I listen to the trees, the living sacred trees,
and know that this bird needs a cage.

Haiku

what makes you
fill my diary with your
interests?

Snake

Snake silently slinks
in the dark cave of life;
in discomfort,
sliding beneath
rocks, through stones.

A frustration of
old skin bursts,
the old discarded, dispossessed.

Not to be rehung,
wardrobed,
and looked on dustily,
memory clinging as
shards of skin cling,
in irritation, withering.

An act of atonement
is made,
a gift is given,
a scraping clean
of the scene.

Snake emerges
into sunlight, warmth.
Basking glory
in new skin,
a growth within.

Airbrushing the Sun Installation

The sun, its resolute radiance
in primaeval yellow hue, sees no shadows.
Its steadfast beam airbrushes tarnish
from our existence, as does the man who
sees his life through a video camera.
Long lensed, the camera sharpens and intensifies,
for life's grubby fingerprints
leave no marks on the celluloid,
and the constant reruns are convincing in their acceptability,
leaving only a screen's depth of perfection; a transparency.

The wintry gleam falls on sunbathers
wrapped in coats and fleecy scarves, spreadeagled in unreal light,
basking in their own narcissistic reflection.
They play to a full house,
for in their mind's eye
they are the sun.
They are indeed the holy one.

Butterfly Wing

Butterfly wing
one day exulting the glory of the light
another in tossed abandon,
fearless in the storm, letting go.

Every year there's a demonstration
of rebirth and growth
when sustaining clues abound,
(how the years slip by unnoticed).

> The wind chime of last year's ash keys;
> the dead purple of last year's catkins;
> the drifting of last year's leaves.

Storms rage on the surface
far away from this exultation,
tearing the top layers of mind,
ripping craters in the fearsome waters.

Butterfly wing flutters
falters, caught in the fight.
Then sinking, slowly absorbed
into the depths,
the deep blue depths
of peace.

Here will the butterfly child wait
caught in the transient moment

locked out, unprepared for this,
attendant on another chance;
life in the glorious sunlight.

> Green budburst inexorably explodes;
> pulsating wing stretch unfolds;
> pumping breath stream implodes.

Haiku

put my news
in the diary of your thoughts;
memory

The sacrifice

In the primaeval swamp of
the uncreated, know only
God's breath breathes.

He beats the heart,
and with our fingers he touches
his world. In our eyes he sees
the distortion, and our ears are his
to hear whatever
is near.
Pray in the midst of
the prayer that his words
are there, the enabling
to share, the expression,
the care.

A Brief History of Time and The Secret of The Universe Explained

A brief history of time in all its infirmity,
comes down to only one convincing reality,
and that is Now and Now is Eternity.

The secret of the universe has only one certainty,
that is death; a step out of time's tenancy
into Life, Creation and perpetual omneity.

Haiku

cold turkey Christmas;
mind grapples for
reinstatement

Sunday Morning in Bishop's Cleeve

Does the village church bell
toll at ten?
And will the local Tesco
open then?

The clear blue air rings
a belling chime,
the queue outside awaits
the time

when the doors are flung
open wide
and hungry hordes
pour inside.

Across the car park from
corners four
the hurrying figures
arrive instore.

Shopping trolleys snatched,
wheels adrift,
bags and bulging wallets but
spirit thrift.

"Attention: this is a customer
announcement,
I have to make a profound
pronouncement.

The 7th aisle is where
you'll find
sustaining food of a
different kind.

A sale is on; stocks will never
run low;
it's all quite free; and it all
must go."

The cry goes up, "The shelves
are bare!
Let's complain; we'll look
elsewhere!"

But all else is cluttered with
expensive distractions,
They might well look inside and check
their reactions,

Then return to this, the empty
seventh aisle
and fill their baskets with each
other's smile.

Does the church bell
toll at ten?
And will your local Tesco
open then?

The one

I am the one
who collects
cascades of stars,
bagging them
in next year's memories.

I am the one,
who at Christ's next birth
will open minds and
pour stars in their abundance,
as sleep dust,
dreamful of radiance
cascading recollection.

I am the one
who cuts down kisses
to cast on the
fire of forgetfulness.

I am the one
whose thoughts on
earthquakes, ethics and other things
are sent into the universe
of already knowing.

I am the one
whose fear finds fullness
in the missing heartbeat,
whose absence teaches
recollection.

I am the one
whose favourite fantasy
resides in a cloud of unknowing;
a cloud of stardust;
a cloud of last year's memory.

Haiku

autumn leaves
collect in a frosted hollow;
your mind

Education

A small girl in her new school dress
of bright green checks
entered the 'big school' classroom
filled with awesome desks.

The world was ready to assault her;
she hesitated, then faltered
for she knew her secret treasure
needed nurture, not torture.
The unripe kernel was torn from the fruit
and buried, wishfully never to be found,
under a tree in the school playground.

Concealed and encased in the broken shell only,
she learned to enact the required hollow bit parts
from worldly scenes, shallow and lonely.
This much school taught her.

A failed actress would one day flee the world
and find the child returning;
her heart's desire re uniting
with the unearthed treasure.
Her secret longing would, at last,
find blessed refuge in unworldly pleasure.

Where I come from

A memory emerges
from the family trapped in the faded album
of a lost place
deep in the heath land
with hot heather-feeding bees
and tall Pooh-like trees.
(When best friends came home with me,
I'm sure there was always honey too for tea).
A day dreaming time of unworldliness;
a feature which school failed to address.

Then floating, face up, in tropical waters
caressed and blessed in the mirage
of a merciless African sun;
and that sun took me to another spot
where midnight leopards crept, spotless or not.
Baboons roamed unfenced around the house;
the cat brought in snake instead of mouse.
Mangoes picked, juices dripped
down our palms and up our arms.

Fond memories of the River Ouse
beside which I began to muse;
college scarves and cherished times
picking words from foggy days, finding rhymes.

Mosquito nets and air conditioning
in yet another global repositioning;
brown sugar beaches and coconut palms
inspired the soul with tropical balm.
Where do I come from? I hate to say,
but if it comes to an immediate crisis,
a vague "Oh, here and there," suffices.

The Service

Order of service, specs and candle,
Common Prayer Book and juggled hymnal.
*"On this day shall be said
orisons for the living dead . . ."*
        Where does spirit lie?
        Which page, where?
Find it amongst
intoned response and recited prayer.

Psalm eighty six, chanted song,
find hymn number *one hundred and one.*
        Where's the soul in this
        service of eternal bliss?

Glasses off, glasses on,
rifled pages scatter on stone,
wax burned fingers search for coins,
miss the note of the modern version,
lose the place in this holy coercion.
        Where's the peace, where the heart?
        When does meditation start?

Stage struck sonorous Bible choices
intoned by glooming holy voices;
a grim angel carries the cross;
divine honours are paid;
and deification is made
of love and loss.

A faithful few
in the back pew
make petition for me
make intercession for you . . . .
Perhaps the answer comes on page ten?
       The transient moment before pious amen.

Meeting

I come
in insignificance
to meet
you here.

The
broken bench
an anchor
for my
raging mind.

soul

The bench V

The
known
way

to
the bench
on the edge
of it

I may go
without hesitation

to rest
as the wind speaks
and passes by
glistening my head
with
water

The walk

The climb is not without difficulties
after an innocent start when she was
unknowing of the fulfilment,
the way is rough, edge clinging.

Her one desire is to attain apical
perspectives of detachment

Walking through the vaulted branches
wind-creased decorated columns, evergreen,
the cathedral floats above the earth,
an aspiration in stained glass skies.
Silence held the living spaces; private chapels of rest,
while all outside is unreal; of peripheral interest.

Then there is a sign.
Three ways: On, Back or The Peak.
That last proves stony and fenced;
when emergence suddenly,
and all is revealed;
total circumference accomplished.

The ascent had been effortless;
a flight from enormity to obscurity;
she became just one small part
of the great upsurge of life blood,
the great smiling love that defies gravity.
From her elevated position
she is lord of the earth and sky
for all below appears unimportant
and she knew she was but a fragmented shred
of this Great Insignificance,
whereupon transcendence descends to immanence.

Marks

I can move through life
leaving no footprint
making no sound.
The path I tread
does not
shake the world
or
move the heavens.
My silent progress
is one of harmony
with the order of things.
A faint
resonance
is all I leave,
a current of air,
perhaps a memory
or even a prayer.

The now empty room
is a testimony
to this.
They have taken
their imprint
which so disturbed
the space
leaving only
an echo
or even just
a trace
of love.

Sea

The sea the sea
the deep blue sea
is constantly
calling
from its transparent
depths.

The fish pass
through it.

And in my
transparency
the cry of the bird
passes through me
for I am
formless.

Door II

In our light
he brings me
to the door.

We separate.
He has gone into
the blinding,
into the
sacred light.

He takes
the fire
to place
in our breast
lovingly

and in his palm
he holds
the flame
he holds
the blessing
tenderly.

Under cover of darkness

The hope that dwells under darkness cover,
the shroud of the night
that loving fills;
the love that drives the purpose, exalts the living
and powers the will.

The limit living expectancy of mine
once incisive with dangerous excitement at the
cutting edge of time;

this power no longer takes my hand
but leaves me on a blunted knife-edge
of loving demand.

I turn to earthy patient labour,
unhurried, mindfully done as offering must.
It is offered up, not for any grace or favour
but to be simply held, in heavenly trust.

Summer comes

And now that spring, at last, is here
and restful awareness
awaits, briefly,
the season to bloom.

Now that the steepled view,
taken from the ashen security,
is faintly obscured
but full of love.

Now that the living memory
rests in peace
and unity of the spirit
where trust and faith
have not been broken,

then the soul awaits, too,
for the abiding presence
in love to grow into;
to flower.

Test

In a honeysuckled life,
one not enduring flailing and torture,
fight, or poverty;
one that does not wipe dusty, tear stained flies
from innocent faces,
or find its beloved, in death,
amongst the tyrant's victims.
One that does not crumple last night's bedding
into the paper bank,
or pull the needle of forgetfulness
from swollen veins,
or clutch bony fingers to
a vacancy behind its ribs.

For this lack, youthful cries admonished
This life has not suffered!
Only in ideas of subtraction
hopes are thereby entertained
for the grace of compassion.

The portal

He is the doorkeeper
to the portal
which opens the way.

He awaits
the approach.
In fearsome trepidation
she comes before
his mindful presence
in her being.

"It's alright
it's alright
you may use me
your love will do."
The whispering wing beat
flies through.

She is in fearful amaze
for was it not written so?
Where is her own
whispering heartbeat?

She hears it go,
tear stained,
in shaming awe
humbly into unknowing.

Where will he be?
Where will he be?

What works in her?
Works also in he.

Silence

In silence
reverential.
A trembling flash,
admittance
in the blink of an eye.

The wind is in silence
as it passes through.
The rain is in silence
as it falls
into the space of you.

String theory

No equation this,
for circles of light descend
threading heart and soul
to spirit, weaving
threads of light, vibrating
pulsating light
in the star filled night,
clothing
clothing
with glory.
Blessed is that night
when clothed in light.

Stone

Dark stone
hard from earth's profundity
    Guide me
cleansed
by unfathomable oceans
    Heal me
tempered and
sand smoothed
    Touch me
so solid stone
vibrant living core
    Hold me
marbled stone
shot through with light
    See me
living stone
ancient stone
      I live in your soul
      Your soul throbs in me

The cloud of unknowing

The manifestation
of the unmanifest.
The creation
of the uncreated
dwelling in the silence
of the single clapped hand,
or the voiceless cry
lost in space;
resonating the sound of thunder
beating on heaven's
invisible door;
tearing at the
insubstantial veil of darkness
that surrounds all.
The kiss subliminal
that engages with nothing
but the emanation
of the unknown.
Only in silence
knowing you
as you are
I am.

Route Finder

Do I need a map?

For when the road ahead is brilliantly lit
and inky tree shadows
deeply veil the path,
I see threaded beads of light
scattered, illuminating a passage
through dark shades of unknowing.

Here I find a hesitant, fearing
heart entertaining insecurities,
but stepping into the bright clearing
of conscious light, they vanish.

There I find obdurate resistance
lying in self-righteous response,
and disentangling compulsion from acceptance,
follow the scintillation instead.

Then I find harboured pain
tightly tethered, safely nurtured,
raised from the dead once again
and trusting the light to lead me on

I find I do not need a map.

Sea storm

The gale of the world
pours across grey Atlantic wastes
taking spume off wave ridges
hurtling in to turbulent
wing torn tossed screeching.
Rain driven smashed against
the merciless pounding
rocks picked and cracked
smoothed fragility in the face of it.

The exciting breath screams
and torn from the voiceless mouth
the cry is lost
- oh my people grieve not -
your burden is lifted in the joy and peace
of the sheltering night,
at the centre, the heart-warming centre.
For standing together, with a sword in each hand,
we rend the storm with our immobility.

He, the Christ, will be within
behind, beside, before; invincible
in the fearsome immensity of the world.
Together, we will cleave
the mystery of our soul.

The past

The thieving accuser comes
to show me my shallow innocence,
for I too once was thief.
And in my self-righteous purity
I see my past mistake.

The small bird
beats herself against a
dark outside window
in desperation for light;
to be seen in her intention to escape
her prison. For she was caged once,
and the sin imprisoned.

The guilty wounds were borne
on her minute face
and to find the light now, the remorse,
she beats against my glass heart
and I hold her tenderly
up to the light within,
aware of my guilty sin.

Wind

When you listen to wind
faintest leaf twist
rising falling
coming crescendo
falling spilling
taking stillness
out of leaves
tugging breaking
no beginning.

When you feel wind
passing by
touching cheek
rising rushing
scattering through trees
touching dropping
lifting those falling
holding fleeting.

When you follow wind
mindfully fading
to silence to stillness
homing
rising falling
no catching
no holding
no ending.

Cry

I cry
to the trees
a wilderness
of trees.
I cry
in my
aloneness
for I am
nothing
and nothing
is me.

Abraham and Isaac

      Or was this how Elija felt?
Had he eaten the bread,
drunk the wine
and wondered why?
Climbing alone up to the sacrificial stone,
derelict, in a wilderness of trees,
      was this how Elija felt?
Was his deep despair and sorrow
teaching his soul of human frailities
and in a confusion of weariness
was he casting himself on the mercy
of the hill top world?
Did he, too, weep desperate tears
upon discovering his true solitude?
A lamentation in no man's land,
a screaming into the void
when he realized none other was left;
no other was there, he was bereft.
      Is this how Elija felt?
Did he hide his face in shame
at the enormity of his infirmity?
Had it been made plain
that he was nothing of himself
but incapable, lost and empty?
      Is this how Elija felt
when an ocean roared through the leafless bough;
a tsunami engulfing the empty shell
of his soul abandoned in the flooding,
where, in the unformed idea, is creation.

The trees are so present, so still. . . .
'You have work to do, my friend.
Get up, go down from the hill.'

Leaving Home

The departure gate -
such a final state.
There's no going
back of beyond
down that track -
no turning back.
The hustling queue
pushing me through
the open door
which I stood before.
There's no return flight
at this time of night.
Such a final state -
the departure gate.

"Go with the flow,"
they say (those who know)
"This is the way,
no need to pay,
jump straight in,
enjoy the swim."
But what if I drown?
"No; just go
with the flow."
Such a final state
this departure gate.

I could take to the sky
and fly, I thought,
go to the open door
where I stood before,
spread my wings
(such cumbersome things),

jump outside
into the wide
blue yonder.

Of course, it's possible I may fall
and miss the final call
for the departure gate -
such a final state -
that final flight
into the night.

Surrender

You talk of surrender
(thereby hangs a poem).
Surrender to the moment of listening
      when all around is still.
Surrender to one step taken at a time,
      an agonising ascent of the hill.
Surrender to the waiting for a train
      to take you where you will.

Surrender to the long dark corridor
      between there and here.
Surrender to your desperate impatience
      in the face of your fear.
Surrender to the calling feeling
      to sit with you near.
Surrender to dangerous living
      in the poetry of here
      and now
          the fullness of giving.

Soul light

Where does my soul go?
What mysteries does it keep?
in the dark silent watches,
in the mystery of the deep.

What does my soul care?
What matters come from thought,
from energetic fields
flung from the cosmos and caught

out of universal space
by the fleeting of time
and left with only memories
of limitless love divine.

How does my soul teach?
But cloaked with love and shielded by peace,
illumined by truth light
all worldly troubles cease.

Go flow

The glistening road
follows away
sparking light and water
flowing that way
I follow
flowing away.

Other pilgrims travel
the tree lined trail,
eddying, converging in a clearing space,
finding still waters
in a silent growing place.

Here, on the tree of life
hang thoughts of love; that within
more enduring than time's strife,
when the agony of the crucified flees.

In apocryphal fluidity
turn again and turn again
to face your fear and fall to your knees.

Then ride with me, ride with me
in the fullness of time, willingly.
Ride with me,
along the glistening road
to full time liberty.

dreams and visions

Door

A door
ajar
light
emanating

He passes
through
with
backward glance
at me

I am
rooted

Tent

The apexed tent
awaits, door ajar
for three wise men
to come from afar.
The dark interior
is an unknown call
the portal through which
the mind may fall.
These three came
their gift unknown:
their benefice
their affirmation
their spirit.
Concentrated, made one here
and directed out
to the atmosphere.

Empty Rooms

Empty rooms, attics, gable ended
are dust desolate, darkened.
Untidy beds in accommodating rows,
roughly made,
shabby in eiderdown coverings.

The nursery is strangely vacant,
lonely is the small icon
of an unformed child, shrouded,
placed on a doll's dias
in the middle of this narrow forgotten room;
the room with window, without view.
The child awaits recognition.
They will not look. They turn away.

The empty rooms need purification.
The grimy floors are unsuited
to those who walk barefoot.
These shabby empty rooms need clear spaces.

The housekeeper reaches out
towards the window
and turns the blind.
Light floods in,
blinding light
for those who dare to walk barefoot.

Travellers

The travellers wait in tree shade,
staves in hand,
dogs at foot.
The silent sun drenched
afternoon is motionless.
They watch and wait
for the call to
make their move.

The cradle of Africa
holds this stillness.
Where are the crossroads
in this vast unfamiliar sky?
Where will they go?
Where will they fly?

Door III

The woman
enters
pack on back
purposeful
in thinking
the moment is unwatched.

"Let me take
your bag,"
he said softly.

Even in her hesitation
she knows
she cannot
go in
with it.

She comes
to herself.

She slips the pack
from her back.
He takes
the weight.

"Who are you?"
she asks.

"I am
the doorkeeper,"
he said.

Graduation

A narrow bare hotel room
somewhere near the sea
is assigned to me.
I stand centrally
wondering what to do.
Why has no one brought my bag?
Am I to rest here?
I know this room is not mine,
I am here temporarily
in a waiting room.
A place of transition.

Now I see how I am dressed -
the old school uniform
a little incongruous
on these child lost shoulders.

I wait here in uncertainty.
At my time of life
I want to do away with the uniform.
But what will replace it?
Where is my bag?
Nobody brings it.

I have to take initiative.
The responsibility is mine.
Am I supposed to fetch the bag myself?
Will my home clothes still fit?
I thought I no longer needed the bag.
If I remove this apprentice garb
without fetching the bag
       I will be naked
          for there is nothing in the room.

I go for the bag,
> my tie, only, removed.
> Nobody pays me attention;
> neither the receptionist, nor the bystanders.
> A drop falls into the ocean.
> A lantern is made safe, beam obscured.
>
> Perhaps I am not yet ready.

Attack

Imprisoned in my own home,
trapped in the castle quite alone
while, under cover of darkness,
all without is a threat.
Out there lies anarchy.
In the gloom, warmongers lurk, their troops amass;
thieves and murderers plot my overthrow.
My castle is under siege,
the palace in peril.

An unknown friend comes to help
He takes my vulnerable hand to the window
and we look out on the dark forces,
filled with flashing lights and noises
of impending attack.
He laughs.
He laughs at the evil intent,
He renders it impotent.

Mantle

The grieving mother mourns
her new born love.
Her all consuming grief
meets my own bewildered sorrow
in selfless agony, wrapt thus, our tears
fall on the same cheek.

(And when there was life
there was love for you too.
He gave you hardly time to turn around in,
child of light, did you see the Lord
and touch the universe? Did you?

And when the sun shone
there was laughter in it too.
They gave you gentle smiles
to cling onto.
They loved you and lost you,
child of light, child of the universe).

Our tears fall on the same cheek,
the cheek of the tortured Christ,
who, at the moment of death, offers comfort
in an angelic ascension of bodily sacrifice
consuming my prayer to keep me,
keep me in the loving embrace;
for no greater love has man
whose angel's wings,
in protective shielding,
enfold me and behold me.
Behold the man;
behold the lamb.

Dreams

Are you sleeping still cradled in fleecy comfort?
He has entered dreams . . . such dreams.
He has shown vast oceans and wild expanses,
towering Hawaiin waves, rolling through Pacific distances.
He guides open topped tours through vast creations,
faded Havana tenements, and jungled, lost civilisations.
He has touched sight with awesome visions
trembling on the edge of insignificance.
His whispering thought is a fleeting beating in the heart,
a still small voice on the verge of inconsequence.

He leads world adventures to free flowing waterfalls
plunging unendingly into clouded depths,
and to resistant, unclimbed mountainous regrets.

He comes, a backlit intensity, arms outstretched,
and suddenly with clarity, we see
with the door open wide
we have been looking the wrong way:
from the other side!

Then he'll send a solemn teacher
to turn the dreamy tables,
create a space within our temple walls.
He will tell us now is not the time
for toss away tears or flippant remarks;
free choice is out and, joking apart,
this man has come expectantly
to hear news of the Holy Trinity.
We can tell him how, in his presence,
what was once separate we now combine
peace, love, spirit as one.

This is the wisdom residing
in the hollow space of our heart,
and standing humbly empty,
we become trustees of the light.

Enfolded thus, there is exchange;
an intangible essence creates
a vapour in the mist of a November fog;
the warm caress of a skin-touched sunbeam;
the pervasive light in a Turner sunset;
a shock of fragrance lingering by pale winter blossom;
the float of air through the white owl's feather
or the haunting cry of geese hanging frozen in starlight;
the sweet frequency of a blackbird's soft song;
or the honeyed love of the shared tea ceremony.

Or, passing comprehension, the enormity
of the all consuming earth in continental collision
and the regeneration of the deep sea trench plunging to the centre.
Spinning air streams, in ferment,
tornados tearing our insubstantial lives,
uprooting, casting out, terrifying breath of life.
The day star ablaze with energising light falling to earth.
The watershed outpouring, flooding, nourishing,
feeding the living, breathing, sun kissed abundance.

Hear this
in the creation lies art.
Thought is art.
Thou art heart,
Thou art.

Hear:
Thou art,
Thou art heart.

The valley path

With her daemon dog, faithful friend
engrossed in exploration of a different sensuous world,
from home to dark wood of unknowing,
their valley path is a daily going.
Ensnaring crouching bramble,
as a lion with furtive throaty rumble,
awaits in the encroaching tangle.

Distracting fly tipped fetters
make a daily impediment;
time wasting patient removal
in seeking the well worn way,
for this sort of thing happens every day.

Her dog, in its own universe,
runs headlong to the deep dark wood
and is gone.
Anxiously calling,
the spirited companion unheeding
in the awareness, straining senses silent.
Without warning, unseen,
the shadow rejoins
nose to ground,
ear to sound,
hearts to home,
homeward bound.

Held in God's gaze: The chase

Who ran through my dream?
A sea of silver seeded globes
scattering heads floating airborne
in the wake of fleeting feet.
Where was that happiness running to?
Up up and away.

Making chase, coursing, wild eyed,
not seeing wood for trees
he leaves me tumbled out
at God's feet; he flees.

I am trapped in that fearful unknowing space
to feel, in my heaving breath,
His Presence.
He is as still as stone;
holding me, hare-like,
in servient thrall;
I do not speak, only await his call;
filled with desire to know,
I dare not look on His face,
yet I dare not go.

My graven God,
cold in remote awesome splendour,
comes alive when I,
in unknowing Trust, surrender.

My childlike need
melts His heart.
Mine melts in His.
We shall not part.

angels

Stone Butterfly

A butterfly child, locked in stone on
wind tossed cliff top, waits.
Silver glints on wave
blown in off ocean stretch;
light sparking
tossed out from
purple sky glooming
hastens landward;
candy striped columbine
surf haze shelters there
on fluttering wing
in the sea's wild roar;
the wave creates
and is gone in returning
breaking the stone,
releasing life.

Awake

Awake! Awake!
Alarm bells are ringing,
waiting saints in communion singing.
He is coming this way,
and is planning to stay.
Bestir yourselves,
attend to him,
make ready a room,
let him in.

This way he comes,
let him pass,
for we do not go there
He comes to us.
He comes to turn over tables,
lay them bare,
make room enough to fill the air
with love.

Graceful acceptance
is our return,
To do his will
is what we learn.
Awake your dreams,
put them aside,
he comes, in resonance,
with what's inside.

Loneliness

"Everything went wrong after that."
The old woman's recollection,
of untimely loss, still so keenly felt.
Sorrowing old eyes
permitting only the briefest glimpse
at the long loneliness
of her rocking chair years.

And the listening ears so powerless
to make right the grief
to lift the burden,
the back crumpled
from the weight of it.
What is left?

Companion

He is behind directing
and he is before leading.
He walks the step,
he moves the pen.
He watches.
He is the light
against which life is held,
the Christ inside
the vision.
He translates the love.
He waits,
listening to the thoughts,
for the understanding,
for his time.
Movements are made for him.
He beckons.
He takes the power away
and makes it his.
He guards the emotional knot
awaiting its release.
He untangles,
he holds the loose ends.
His transference is slowly wise,
leaving clues, patiently,
to the stumbling blocks
in the path.
He leaves the work to be done.
He is waiting.

Net

He casts his net daily
awaiting a bite expectantly.
He sees more in us
than we know of yet.
(There are stranger things
in heaven and earth).
He sows the seed
of self-belief,
not knowing where
response will come.
The growth
of new consciousness
the bursting love of life
unfolding,
for many kindred sparks
are kindled
in his blazing light.
And then the blossoming
bears fruit
the seed is set
anew. Meanwhile
he continues to cast his net.

Ghost

The butterfly child
waits daily at this quiet corner
driven from the road hell
where she no longer belongs.

She lives on a 'wing and a prayer'
caught in the moment,
behind time -
a painted lady
hoping for release,
an unfolding from
the encasing chrysalis.
Waiting for rebirth
her living to end.

Haiku

Scattering of children
tumble seawards;
life littered beach babies.

Beach Life

In pairs we walk, the space inside
constantly companioned, lovingly held.
Some with dogs at foot
others push chaired into the wind;
some tethered to the sky
by friendly tugging kites.
Some chasing footballs,
others bowled over and stumped;
Many with backpacked valuables
full of needs perceived; shoulder borne.
Perhaps walking sticks or
staffs hand clasped;
mobile phones pressed to ears,
or cameras witnessing locked in moments;
driftwood thrown downwind,
whisking barking spirits.
Smiling and heart grasped
in pairs we walk.

A few there are
who walk alone amongst us
wearing New Life tee shirts.
They are the empty handed
not even pocketed in their simplicity,
and leaving firm and faithful followed footprints
they pass on by.

November 11th

Whispers of death
in an autumn sacrifice of golden falling
and jumbling one above the other;
bronze hewn, red bloodied
or parchment yellow, rotting, skeletal;
faint breathing spirits
in their last gasp.

Each year the memory feeds the next,
the trapped ancient sunlight
releasing back into renewal.
For when the light glints
on the sacrificial death pile
a glory is witnessed;
A shining powerful glory
seen in the woods, in the fields,
under trees, smothering the sun blest earth.

Speak to these soldiers through the ethereal tracery
of their passing,
a ghostly mist absorbing the words……
The dying whisper comes back,
"We, too, were blessed,
for we lie in peace
wrapped in this cloth of gold."

The golden marigold

Diffusing a dark situation of self absorbtion
with the light of its presence,
a golden marigold, in its simplicity,
looks up at the world.
It is;
it is waiting;
a radiant humility of beauty love and light;
waiting for fulfilment in loving response.
It craves appreciation.
God's work is done.
In his illumined presence,
in the transient nature of its divinity
God's work is done.

Incase, lost in dark moments,
the meaning is missed today,
presence is summoned again and again;
each passing hour
each divinely created beauty shouts
Here I am, look at me!
Is that not enough?
Here I am again . . . and again . .
Praise Him!

Cufflinks

Cold pre-Christmas pavements dusk light
in the homeless haven of his cleanly laundered shirt,
face unmirrored grimy hair mat.
Open sleeves conceal cold hands in confusion,
for he has no cufflinks.

I have no cufflinks to give.
This unbuttoned haven was found behind the Open Door,
somewhere near the Centre.
I make a mental note to find that place.
When the rush is over,
the shopping done,
the children collected,
supper cooked,
Christmas connected,
I will look for the Open Door . . .
but he is the here now which I stand before,
is he now here the open door?

I have no cufflinks.
I make a promise to give the bearer hug.
We hug an exchange in the dusky glow
of his pavement Christmas chill.

You are there

In my silent meditation
you are there.
In my inner conversation
you are there.

In every loving feeling
and in every human dealing
you are there.

In my going and my staying
you are there.
In my hoping and my praying
you are there.

I find you when I need you,
you help me and you feed me
for you are there.

You are there in every move I make.
You share in every breath I take.
You fill my soul with fire,
my heart with loving desire
for you are there.

You are with me when I fall asleep
and ever present when I rise from the deep.
You are there in the words I write,
I paint pictures for your delight.

In my reading, the recitation
is said for you.
In my being any hesitation
is a thought of you.

Whenever my spirit flies free
I show you all the things I see,
for you are there.

I find you when I'm all alone
for you are there,
and in my weak-willed efforts to atone
you are there.

In everything, I share,
for you are there,
you are there.

Haiku

winter intensity
when wind will cease; faint cries heard;
iced whispers only

Who blesses the vicar?

I wonder, who blesses the vicar?
You'd think his trip to heaven would be much quicker
with the angelic care that's due to him
to prevent his halo from getting dim.
With all those Saints watching his soul,
heaven would seem a simple goal.
Also, if prayers are said on his behalf,
he'd find it possible to raise a laugh
with congregational whims
to sing hands up holy hymns.
Thus songs would carry him to a higher realm
where his spirit would happily overwhelm
him in his need to rest
in a lonely holy quest.
As the Bishop has his interests at heart
it gets him off to a flying start;
and with all those Bible readings taking effect
his thirsty soul will never suffer neglect.
By these means his trip to heaven
should be much quicker, but
ask yourselves, who blesses the Vicar?

love and fear

This word

This word that came
that day
was love.
This birthing amazement
which drew them in
was love.
This star that shone from
cold clear space
was love.
This lamb that bleated
in fragile warmth
was love.
This donkey that carried
her here
was love.
This golden resting
in stable straw
was love.
This gift we bring,
this heartfelt offering
is love.

Tree Worship

Damp fragrant earth
steaming in sun warmth.
Emerging life
hungering for light.
How many times am I summoned here?
Yet I still question.
A homecoming.
It is almost tropical in the birdsong,
the dripping, thirsting wetness.

I stand before and open my heart.
If I were to worship
it is here
it is when our melting bellies touch.
It is here now,
with arms encircling
sap rising energy.

Sheep

Who is wolf?
Who is sheep?
Sheep's foot stamping assertion;
power over wolf.

Wolf, limbs braced and poised,
lip snarled,
tooth bared,
eye intent
on the soft throat
tasting blood.

Sheep's oblong eyes,
fearful, but assertive
in her pregnancy;
protectively curious.

Squaring up
sheep kissed wolf
and wolf fled.

Ode to a Deer

In your stillness
you are at one with your creation.
Your silent step and vigilant
attention to the moment
in awareness of detail;
the grass blade, the fallen leaf,
the bud on twig tip,
the aerial dance of mayfly
in slanting evening light.
A lesson in meditation.

Living with death on your shoulder
your fear manifests
only at times of threat,
because as I sit watching
your innocent route
through the woodland,
you observe me
but perceive no danger.
Indeed I am no threat.
The fear rests in your heart
as uncertainty causes alarm.
Adrenalin; fear floods
the unconscious memory scent
of wolf.

You flee.
Bounding spirit.

Duck

Drake approaches duck
with amorous intent
(Intent to preach love in hope
that duck will relent).
She has no interest in his overtures
and rebuffs the pleading lament.
His retreat is wise
for there is no welcome present.
His feathers ruffled,
he shakes them out, settles,
and washes away the non-event.
He looks about with fresh intent.
Surely, not all ducks will hold
for him such contempt?

Home Flight

The aircraft dips its wing
in graceful descent, allowing
perfect vision,
in a cloud gapped moment ,
of homeland.

Love pours through, pierced
gold rimmed clouds of unknowing.
Raindrops glisten in eyes which
 look back in memory to see
the broken window
(truck reversing),
the open door
which we stood before,
the bridge spanned space
between fear and grace,
the bench
which was there
always to share.
Tears of love
rain through.

Summer afternoon

My heart bursts for you,
and transposed here now in the air
moving across skin in soft caress,
in the ripple on the still calm lake;
the evocation of a coot call
falling out of silence;
the diligent bee feeding in pink clover;
hawkbits, scabious and wild grasses
moving in the sound of the beech leaves turning.

By these ways you call me back
and we sit back to back.
An imaginary sharing of silence
resting in you; you in me.

Roe Deer

Roe deer
springs clearing
from the trees unknowing
for the watcher is silent.
Watched, he hesitates
in his stillness
he looks back
unsure of what he sees.
He scents fear. He flees.

Haiku

everything depends on
love energy directed
to rebirth

Tenderness

Tenderness
(at the beginning of understanding)
fills them with compassion.
Desiring to touch;
an unfolding caress,
as soft summer air strokes
the face of the beloved.
Feeling tendrils reaching out
enfolding the melting heart.

Held in each other
the sun bathes them
in its warmth,
light penetrating
the centre of their being.

Their tenderness
is a fragile love
absorbed and sacred.
It rests at the centre
it sends searchlights,
it penetrates their soul.

Love lost

I return to this notebook
where once the fire took my pen,
your spirit filled me fully then.

This page is empty of desire
and my unrequited heart burns;
an empty place where there are no returns.

I am in a cold place –
the recess of your heart.
I fear this will forever be my cross
for the painful resonance I feel is loss.

A sword pierces that which you see
and what you see is resilience,
paper thin.
Twist it in.

Memories

Sometimes, looking on the simplest of things
can bring a flash of such exquisite joy and love
that the heart leaps in ecstasy
and memories flood through a time
when I was not too shy
to feel like embracing the world.

A time when it was okay to lie
squinting idly at scudding cloudy sky;
or to walk barefoot with sandy toes
on the edge of ice cold ocean floes,
the shirt tucked into trouser band
as if by some other careless hand,
the hair erect in tousled spikes,
defiant from ravages of sleepless nights.

A moment when a drop of water reflected a world of light,
spangled, like some celebration, across the sky at night;
or flower children picking cowslips from the fields was no worse
than planting them in the cosmic life force of the universe.
Those times when dream chance gave opportunities not to be missed,
of meeting unrequited lovers when my lips were kissed and kissed and kissed.

I remember that day I awoke to see a pale mist dawn,
like a wet watercolour, barely alive, barely born
and I was not too shy in that time and space
to feel the whole of the human race
take me by the hand and pull me,
pull me into perpetual spin
further up, further up and further in.

Christmas Story

"Now in this city . . . there
is a dwelling place. A tiny lotus flower,
within it a tiny space.
Seek what is within it . . .
As wide as that space outside is the space
Within the heart." (Hindu scripture)

Noise without, bar beer drinker
lager lout, trader, traveller, hustle, shout,
forming queues, exchanging news,
pushing in, city sin.

Out back, behind the bar,
the barn was made ready
for this young lady to find sanctuary;
a quiet place in which to have her baby.
A candle lit shelter from wind and rain,
warmth, rough and ready, a nestling of hay.
Patient donkey, innocent lamb
folded into a winged stillness, waiting,
off stage to bear silent witness
to this miracle play.

Stars shone steadfast, ephemeral light
beaming down upon winter weathered fields.
A night watch of shepherds, ever vigilant,
saw what was missed by
the seething city centre mind;
a heavenly host descending
in a whispering arrival of This Word.

In a holy and pregnant silence
a barn birth occurred, a baby kissed,
a kingdom created from which

all thought and fear had been dismissed.
Light and blessing seemed to surround the boy
as the mother, caressing, held close her secret joy.
A place of peace had been born
from the womb of creation.

The shepherds, unmoved by city life, and curious,
stood before the open barn door:
a welcoming light, beckoning them to
the conscious space within.

They bore Presence in kind.
Looking on the baby
held to the young woman's breast
their hearts opened in a rush of new born love
vanquishing all worldly concerns and
into what had been memory only,
the Christ child within was reborn in them that day.
Unquestioning, unconditional, wordless
and enfolded thus in God's Great Stillness
they knelt.

I am in peace

I am in peace
and you are in me and I am in you,
the cavern of your breast,
a still place, where,
within every porous part,
filtrated in blood,
I enter your very heart.
Enmeshed and blessed
by the web of my desire,
the groaning sap rising flow
quenching a burning, sacral fire,
you lift your weight from me
with soft lips on my brow.
We bear fruit in silent vow.

HAIKU

butterfly trembles
at the window in winter's last gasp
tenderly found

still moments

Three haiku

coming by an
unknown way; sitting to rest warm
spirit caressed

                                              November's grey shadow
                                                  insinuates trees space;
                                                        we gallop through

cry of geese frozen
in the darkness of space light;
dawn fills the sky

Evening

Distant is the roar of the world
as stretching the silent space
beyond the evening window
to this place with you in it.

The shocking evening intensity
of forget-me-not blue
fills in the eye's immensity
and a gasp of breathless wonder,
as lambs bleat painfully
across the meadow,
fearing the night's approach,
calling mother love out from
shadow's lengthening grasp.

The breeze takes chiming foliage
and turns it around
and back, each leaf
brushing another's green heaven
in tune with the wind.

Evening vespers are sung from every branch
when the blackbird comes in final flight
to call softly
goodnight.

Cat

sublime grace
cat landing
feather light
knee bound
weightless
it curls its contentment
lapping comfort
pressing purrs
in arm crook
the comforting caress
enfolds and
rests here
rests here
in the heart

Horse

Equus flies
in graceful
cadenced carriage
bearing his being
waits
not wanting
to touch
but just to be
with me
we stand apart
but
joined in heart
resting here
resting here
in our stillness

Stillness

A petal falls out of time
into stillness.

Bee's wing vibrates
in fragrance.

Spider waits suspended
between a lily leaf
and nothing.

In this now
when just a forgotten memory,
and of inconsequence invisible,
or when will be is now,
speak of stillness.
Teach always to keep
love in eternity.

Spider waits as
bee is caught
in sweet deathless
orange blossom.
Falling petal lies spent
a whisper only
a whisper in stillness.

Sunday moment

Shock of scented
winter blossom
recalling a memory,
left in garden oasis where
a stone Buddha waits
in peace perpetual.
This is the morning when
church bells recall
a presence awakening.
Still heart.
Still mind.
Mindfully wind
speaks through
bough and branch.
In pure light
He shares this
enamelled moment
of clarity.
The calling to
briefly be in it
sharing
transient moment
fading in
gathering gloom
as rain touches heart.
Knowing sunlight
will come again
as it comes for you.
Gathering in the storm
tearing fragile bloom,
life reborn,
messenger of hope.

Lunchtime at Stanton

The stillness captured
by the late summer
fly buzz through memory
of summers gone;
childhood years in ancient sunlight.

Three horses tread softly the track,
their companion watches their passing
with faint interest, ears briefly attuned.

Resting here in the encompassing silence
of soft, leaf touching air;
a skin caressing movement
which takes thistledown in upward float;
sounds ripple across the valley atmosphere;
a distant buzzard calling, but sounding near,
the frantic whine of bees caught in rosebuds;
drone of aircraft; chug of engine in idle gear;
a woodpigeon's sad call to her lost lover;
a voice in loving reprimand
at the tail swishing, hoof stamping demand.

These summer sounds
threaded through
on silver chains,
encircle my senses
welding light air, linking to
the hot gilded terrace,
of stone built house,
the valley full of monumental silence,
untrapped, flowing seaward.

Unheard sounds
from far away lands
encompass our world
and all the spaces between
planets, moons and stars.
The whole of creation
necklaced in a moment
by a silver beaded chain
resting upon my heart.

Two haiku

raindrop twig tipped
a world upside down frozen
suspension

we sit
in this great stillness;
world passes by

The host (with thanks to Wordsworth)

We wandered alone, we two,
when all at once we saw, not few,
but a host of iridescence,
iridescence blue.

The damsels clung in watery crowd
or danced in an exalted cloud
of blue, of blue
of forget-me-not-blue.

Emerging here, emerging there
they flashed and danced in summer air,
caught in a forget-me-not heaven fair
of blue, of blue, of iridescent blue.

Haiku

pink clouds adorning
the sea calm morning
gull waiting reflected in it

Sunday Morning

The back door bangs open
on the stove glow within.
She brings with her the particled air
of cloudless frosted fields,
the brilliant blue cold sharpness
of winter sunlit skies
and an eager fresh-filled heart
full of smiles.

There is a sweet welcoming smell
of hot syrupy oatmeal,
toast and steaming coffee.
The radio is tuned in
to Sunday morning music
and radiant sunshine
slants between curtains onto
breakfast bowls, chinking spoons,
milky frosted flakes
consumed in warmth.

She joins the scene and smiles.
No one looks up.

Haiku

pink iced morning sky
wind torn
fallen leaf scattering

Spring

A flock of last year's leaves
took off in the brisk pre-spring breeze
and flew with rattling song
in the wind-willed air,
past us and into beyond.

A galaxy of sunlight glints across the fields
for each tipped grass blade yields
a sparkling harvest of frost melt;
where hoof prints split the turf
in the shadow of a galloping mare
and notes of cascading birdsong
crack open the morning air.

And then one day it *was* spring,
and the buzzard, in silence, tilts his wing
into the soft mellow uprising flood.

A roe buck, startled in purposeful flight,
bounds across the field and vanishes from sight
into trees, whose buds barely breaking

conceal the kestrel's wild cry of longing care,
whilst butterflies flirt in the pregnant air
illuminated by dappling sunlit beams
heavy with the pervading scent of bluebells,
pungent wild garlic and other woodland smells.

Starry night

Here is a flavour of summer nights,
the sweet juice of midnight
surrounded by stars
in their dark depths
and their light,
holding presence in the soft sultry air,
passing through history
onto our upturned faces.
And the swan flies always
through the milky sea,
always it comes
winging back to me.

Haiku

heron's wide wing beat
across grey reflected reservoir
coot calling

revelations

Come alive

The morning awakes.
Pigeon claps wings
in arcing flight
as if to dismiss
the passing night.

Door IV

Opening the door one end of summer day
I entered a loophole of love
which made me stop, listen and pray

Snowdrops

Each bulb had been carefully placed;
nurtured for some future glorious proliferation.
An interregnum of loss of attention
and the place became swamped and weeded.
Roots had inveigled every colony
with choking forgetfulness.

The clearance, rooting out,
needed painstaking patience
as such gems already in their fulfilment
became uprooted;
disturbance pulled out of the heart.

Slowly the place was cleared,
caressingly lost bulbs replaced,
and hidden purity of flower revealed.
A beam of weak winter sunlight
intensified in the white blossom.

Tiercel

In his stillness the Tiercel hangs
attendant on the moment,
attuned to the raging gale buffet,
which is of inconsequence
to his peace within.

For from his immobility
he casts his eye over the green pasture
and it is fixed on me.

I have run. I have hidden,
but each time he slices the wind
and remains above
in his stillness, in his solitude.

His cry is taken from his belly to his throat
and is caught in the elemental roar.
It pierces and I am frozen.

He descends.
The light falls to earth
in vertical arrow shaft.
I am caught in his shadow
for I no longer see the worldly sun.

And in the agony of surrender
his angelic wings
enfold me in mantling protection.
He breathes,
"Fear not. For I am with you,
here in your heart,
here in the hearts of all. I am."

And in the consuming fire
we become one.
And in the singularity
I am carried aloft in his grip,
fearless, to the heavens.

Dear David

Remember those questions you asked
but would never answer,
those questions you asked
which I couldn't answer?
Of course I know.
Of course I know the answer.

I 'checked into my room
only to find Gideon's Bible.
The Bible, it seems,
answers my dreams'
and those questions
I couldn't answer.
It tells me I know,
of course I know
the answer.

My story I share
it is all laid bare
there, in Gideon's Bible

Blackbird

When the blackbird sang
it was as if
God had opened the throat
and made a portal
through which He could float,
the most sublime of sounds,
the sweetest note.

Astonished, the bird fell silent
and closed his throat
and looked about with listening ear
unknowing it was himself
who raised the presence here,
himself the conduit for the heavenly song,
coming straight from Source,
a place where we all belong.

Air freshener

Damp lustral sunshine
bathes the Peak in light divine.
Hawthorn scent leaves a cleansing trace
in the light-dappled greening space.
A puff of air percolates my blood
and brushes beech leaves, then a flood
takes the perfume in blustering gust
to spin and tumble in atmospheric thrust.
Thus clarified in the freshening air,
an empty vessel is left standing there.

God loves me?

God loves me, I'm told;
an affirmation only, but written in bold!
How can I *feel* this bleak cold
statement that rattles like a skeletal leaf
in the frosted hollow of mindless belief?

God loves me are words they think I should say,
but what shall I do to make them real?
to turn them into caressing touch and loving feel?
I wonder if I love God?
Does the idea work this way round,
or is it a notion far too profound?

Beloved, come to Me in silent communion,
for I am Love itself, therefore make no affirmation.
Your deepest emotion lies in My heart,
what you give to Me comes back in equal part.
Live this truth, learn this lesson,
you'll find My love in loving expression.

Forgiveness

This death that fills
our hearts with grief
forgave.
This suffering that tests
our self belief
forgave.
This torture that pulled
open our fragile heart
forgave.
This sense of loss that tears
our souls apart
forgave.
This cross that stretched
the power of love to bless
forgave.
This enduring that transcended
time and flesh
forgave.
This Christ survived
the man who died
and forgave.

All That Is

One midsummer morning,
immersed in the dawn chorus and a gathering light,
I find my lips are sealed, but the pen will still write.
Like St Francis, I sit in a privileged place,
and look on Eden with eyes of grace.

Taking nectar to feed its queen,
a profusion of flowers are each touched by a humble bee,
which, unknowingly, pollinates an unseen
world of grass, bush and flowering tree.
And the trees here are filled with birds and song,
driven by love to feed their brood
with a plethora of insect food.

And the truth of this moment, with the dog on my knee,
and the wren-scolded cat (a gleam of sun on his back),
this truth is all what is: a world powered by love
(almost inadvertently, it seems).
And in this love peaceful strength lies at the core,
behind the screen of the thought full door.

I saw, in that moment, the mystery of Trinity,
mere words, which had meant not a lot to me,
became the truth which had always lived as my spirit guide,
and love that cloak in which I could hide;
peace became a potent shield
for God's stillness which would, here now, yield
the way through truth to life.

And in this life I find I am free
for I live now governed by this Trinity.
I am only a woman who simply plants the seeds
and the same one who removes the weeds;

I pat the dog and stroke the cat;
I hoover the carpets and shake out mats;
I day dream on wishes
whilst I wash the dishes;
I know the floor needs mopping;
I do the supermarket shopping.
Sometimes I take a cup of tea, stretching and yawning,
into the garden to meet a summer day dawning;
other times I stand quite still and wait;
or I may I sit and contemplate.
I am one who paints God's glory,
and with my pen I write God's story.

And here is the greatest story ever told:
Rebuild my church with hearts of gold.
Rebuild my church in the Trinity,
then release my soul to deathless infinity.

Stairs

In her daily walk of measured tread,
all beyond entertained an inner dread.

Her steps were marked out in caves of limitation,
until one day, in meditation,
she sought to go upward to the unknown height,
as if through a secret door to find the light.

The ease of the next excursion
indicated much less self-coercion,
and when, eventually, it became a way of ease,
she saw the next horizon up above the trees,

and knew, in that moment, there would always be more to find,
and wondered at how she had been so blind,
locked in the deep dark cave of her mind.

Away from her daily walk of measured tread
she found ever new paths to explore instead.

Cancer cure

In the threat of death, a bodily degradation,
a naked exposure, a humiliation.
The surgeon's blade slices forsaken flesh
and finds fear, resistance, emotional stress.

I waited at this cross looking for a turning,
for a road to acceptance and a silent yearning
in the midst of my prayer, for deliverance.

Do I still doubt? Was the challenge real?
Believe that the scars are there
though the wounds have healed.
Put a hand in the disfiguration on my breast -
it is a tangible doubt of life in a body distressed.

And shall I find my freedom on a holy height?
A transfiguration of body and mind in spiritual light?
I open my heart to the wide horizon and infinite sky.
Believe me when I tell you I did not die.
I did not die.

A transfiguration

*"Either come with me
or go back."*

The cliff path seems on the edge of an unknown place,
where, climbing out of her wretchedness and ungrace,
(for he had revealed to her what had always been:
a glorious light reflected in her face),
it is a heavenly homecoming.

A sea fog shrouds her on the cliff top height,
but, God intoxicated, she arrives
between wide horizon and infinite sky
at a point of radiant light.

(Three other flickering souls in one Christ-like flame
had also trekked
and found *their* glory revealed by Him
in the unknowing cloud
of their intellect).

Stilled, (as they had been)
she hears her integrity and intuitive prayer
speak in her heart;
"Listen to me. I am there. I am there."

I will follow

Yes,
I will follow your light
along dark distances
of time and space
into your blazing presence,
and turning,
I will gaze back
down your fiery beam
onto my own
upturned future face.

Yes,
I will go with you
into the wide passages
of uncharted seas
not knowing where we'll land
and I will climb with you
unscaled regions
of mountainous heights
if you'll not let go my hand.

Mike's Trinity: *Death, Disease, Pestilence*
Acceptance, Compassion, Charity

Thieving magpie, causing anguish in the thrush's breast;
why are you here to take these babies from their nest?
Take your cunning ways and fly from here,
how can you live like this with your conscience clear?

> *But I have babies of my own to feed,*
> *and I love them so.*
> *How else should I live?*
> *It's what I do, it's all I know.*

Pestilent fox, where has your beauty gone?
Where your glossy coat and fine black tipped brush?
Hie thee hence, be gone away!
Why do you lie there in the full light of day?

> *I entertained disease,*
> *and hunger drove me here.*
> *My pain throbs in your heart,*
> *seeking compassion, not fear.*

Vile climate, you bring us drought, famine, fire and flood.
Do you sap even this, my very life blood?
Rage rage against the world so empty of bliss.
Where is our help? What is God's purpose in this?

> *Come to Me in your nakedness;*
> *show the world your dead.*
> *Tell it out in silent appeal;*
> *hold out My hand for bread.*
> *Come to Me; ask this of Me;*
> *I seek your giving power instead.*

Tread lightly

Tread lightly
through eternity,
sunlight touching
the graven memories,
long lost in timeless appeal
of silent churchyards.

Tread lightly
into the space
where wind dapples
through trees
rooted in earth and is caught
touching distant cloudless thought.

Tread lightly
in bodily trance
an effortless action
melting clumsy humanity
with sublime divinity.

Here we are in truth.
Find us.

A poem for all people

Who do you say that I am?

I say that you are the truth
    that lives in me.
I say that when I need you
    I look deep into my integrity.

I say that when I let go
    of my personal pain
you take it from me
    to vaporise in that inner flame.

I say that your life is
    the story of my heart
for what lives in me
    is simply yours in part.

I say that you are the light
    which burns in my soul;
you are the prayer and meditation
    that makes me whole.

And in that holy moment
    when we finally convene
I say that you are the one spirit
    who comes in my dream.

Who do you say that I am?
I say that you are God, you are Man.

**Held in God's Gaze
Reprise**

My graven God,
cold in remote awesome splendour,
comes alive when I,
in unknowing Trust, surrender.

I reach up,
a humble spirit
chastening all adult pride.

He lifts the child;
holds the baby to His breast;
but it is in newborn form
that my helpless quest
melts His heart.
Mine melts in His;
we shall not part.

Tiercel II

Carried aloft in our singularity
the Tiercel uttered soft love sounds
in my soul.
I was just to be;
and now, am consumed.

This is my goal! I am food for God!
This is His need; this is how He grows.
I have to concede, my holy task was acceptance
of His love. In consumption I am to become His Essence,
and am to live on in other silent souls,
healing tired spirits, turning heads
to face the Tiercel,
to face righteousness.
God's work will be done.

Then joyously let it come to me when the time is right!
for I am ready now and expectant for that last journey to the light.

Keep watch

Mark 13 v 35-36